MAYA ANGELOU'S GUIDE TO HOPE

50 SIMPLE WAYS TO SPREAD HOPE

Hardie Grant

B O O K S

WAYS TO SPREAD HOPE...

SELF-LOVE 5

BE YOURSELF 27

RISE UP 49

BE THE RAINBOW 91

SELF-LOVE

ONE

LET LITERATURE RESTORE YOU

Literature was Maya's true love. She adored Louisa May Alcott's *Little Women*, Dickens' *A Tale of Two Cities*, Ralph Ellison's *Invisible Man* and Walt Whitman's *Leaves of Grass*.

TWO

TAKE YOURSELF ON A DATE

THREE

LEARN A POEM BY HEART

FOUR

THAT NEW
HABIT, BOOK
OR PROJECT?
JUST
START

FIVE

CAKE
CAN BRIGHTEN
THE SPIRIT

When Maya was expelled from school, her mother's response was to make her a delicious fresh maple cake; it became one of Maya's most enduring and uplifting memories.

LIKE WHAT YOU DO AND LIKE HOW YOU DO IT

SEVEN

LET YOUR FAILURES BUILD YOU UP

EIGHT

SURROUND *YOURSELF* WITH PLANTS, FLOWERS AND LIVING THINGS

NINE

LOVE YOUR BODY, GIVE IT PLEASURE

WRITE TO INSPIRE HOPE IN YOURSELF AND OTHERS

Maya wrote 167 poems, seven celebrated memoirs and two beloved cookbooks, sharing with others with her wisdom, pain, hope and a secret recipe for banana pudding.

ELEVEN

TRUST YOUR GUT

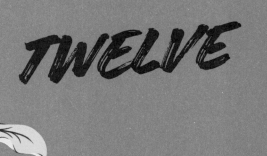

TWELVE

CREATE YOUR LIFE

THIRTEEN

LIVE WHAT YOU TEACH

Maya loved teaching, sharing her great
wisdom and listening to her students.
She gained 55 honorary doctorates in her life.

FOURTEEN

MAKE SPACE: IN YOUR HOME, LIFE AND HEART

FIFTEEN

BE ALL YOU CAN BE

SIXTEEN

LIVE MANY LIVES IN ONE

Maya tried everything and anything, from dancing and diner-cooking, to TONY-winning acting, screenwriting and even releasing her own album *Miss Calypso* in 1952.

NURTURE YOUR CREATIVITY AND HONE YOUR SKILLS

EIGHTEEN

MOVE
YOUR BODY;
BE GRACEFUL,
POWERFUL OR
EXPRESSIVE

NINETEEN

LEARN ANOTHER LANGUAGE

Maya was fascinated by language, from her time touring Europe with a production of *Porgy & Bess*, to her life in Egypt and Ghana; she became proudly multi-lingual.

LIVE WITHOUT REGRET

TWENTY
ONE

BE BRAVE
ENOUGH TO
SHOW YOUR
VULNERABILITIES

TWENTY TWO

BE DISCERNING, INQUIRING AND MINDFUL WITH WHOM YOU GIVE YOUR LOVE

In one of her many speeches, Maya once told young Black women at Spelman College 'I never trust anybody who tells me they love me if the person doesn't love herself or himself.'

TWENTY THREE

DON'T BE AFRAID OF SUCCESS

TWENTY FOUR

LEARN
TO SAY
NO

TWENTY FIVE

EAT SOLO
IN A
RESTAURANT

DARE TO LIVE

In *The Heart of a Woman*, Maya wrote 'I had to trust life, since I was young enough to believe that life loved the person who dared to live it.' In an interview in 1985, at the age of 57, she was happy to say she still believed it.

TWENTY
SEVEN

BE
PERSISTENT

At 16, Maya wanted to work on San Francisco's streetcars but, at first, transport managers wouldn't let her apply. She sat in the office for two weeks until they gave her the job, becoming one of the city's first ever Black streetcar conductors.

TWENTY EIGHT

BE COURAGEOUS; IT'S INFECTIOUS

TWENTY
NINE

TRY A NEW SKILL, EVEN IF YOU'RE AWFUL AT IT

THIRTY

DRAW
POWER
FROM YOUR
FRIENDS, FAMILY,
YOUR ANCESTORS

In 1992, Maya's advice to students facing their first job interview was to 'bring everybody with you that you can remember, who loves you,' for back-up, confidence and inner charisma.

THIRTY
ONE

GROW YOUR COMMUNITY

THIRTY TWO

CHANNEL YOUR ANGER TO WRITE, DANCE, MARCH AND VOTE

THIRTY THREE

JOIN
A CLUB,
A CIRCLE,
A GROUP

THIRTY
FOUR

LEAVE
THE DOOR
OPEN

Remarking on her incredible yet troubled life, in 2014 Maya explained that when young people find themselves with no open doors, they will try to open them themselves by means we might not agree with; we should be generous towards them.

THIRTY FIVE

MAKE
EYE CONTACT,
BE HEARD,
BE
PRESENT

THIRTY
SIX

YOU WON'T ALWAYS BE UNDERSTOOD, AND THAT'S OKAY

I Know Why the Caged Bird Sings remains one of the most celebrated, beloved but consistently banned books in the US, forever causing PTA controversies and its removal from school libraries (and eventually reaching even more readers because of it).

THIRTY
SEVEN

USE
SMALL
ACTS
OF BRAVERY TO
BUILD UP YOUR
COURAGE

THIRTY EIGHT

USE HUMOUR AS POWER;

LAUGH AT THE CRUELTIES OF LIFE

THIRTY NINE

WORK HARD

TO INCREASE

YOUR STRENGTH, PHYSICALLY AND MENTALLY

FORTY

TURN OFF

YOUR PHONE, LAPTOP
AND TV AND

LIVE IN THE

REAL WORLD

FOR AN HOUR

FORTY ONE

PAY
SOMEONE
A COMPLIMENT

FORTY TWO

LET SOMEONE KNOW THEY ARE LOVED

Maya always attributed her successes to the 'rainbows in her clouds': the people whose kindness helped her along the way.

FORTY THREE

SMILE
AT A
STRANGER

FORTY FOUR

OFFER A WARM HUG

FORTY FIVE

ASTONISH OTHERS WITH ACTS OF KINDNESS

FORTY
SIX

WRITE A LETTER TO A FRIEND

FORTY SEVEN

IF YOU CAN,

DONATE

YOUR TIME,

MONEY OR ATTENTION TO

THOSE IN NEED

FORTY EIGHT

CONSIDER KINDNESS AS YOUR LEGACY

On the question of living a successful life and leaving a legacy, Maya memorably said that although people might forget what you say or do, they will always remember how you made them feel.

FORTY
NINE

BAKE
FOR YOUR
FRIENDS,
NEIGHBOURS AND
CO-WORKERS

LEAVE YOUR
FAVOURITE
BOOK
FOR A STRANGER
TO FIND

Published in 2022 by Hardie Grant Books,
an imprint of Hardie Grant Publishing

Hardie Grant Books (London)
5th & 6th Floors
52–54 Southwark Street
London SE1 1UN

Hardie Grant Books (Melbourne)
Building 1, 658 Church Street
Richmond, Victoria 3121
hardiegrantbooks.com

British Library Cataloguing-in-Publication Data. A catalogue
record for this book is available from the British Library.

Maya Angelou's Guide to Hope
ISBN: 978-1-78488-496-3

10 9 8 7 6 5 4 3 2 1

Publisher: Kajal Mistry
Commissioning Editor: Kate Burkett
Editor: Eila Purvis
Design and Art Direction: Studio Noel
Illustrations: Sarah Madden
Text curation: Dan Jones
Production Controller: Katie Jarvis

Colour reproduction by p2d
Printed and bound in China by Leo Paper Products Ltd.

MIX
Paper from
responsible sources
FSC™ C020056
FSC
www.fsc.org